Cooking with Herbs

Healthy and Delicious Recipes with Herbs

Copyright © 2020

All rights reserved.

DEDICATION

The author and publisher have provided this e-book to you for your personal use only. You may not make this e-book publicly available in any way. Copyright infringement is against the law. If you believe the copy of this e-book you are reading infringes on the author's copyright, please notify the publisher at: https://us.macmillan.com/piracy

Contents

Tabbouleh Salad..1
Pesto alla Genovese (Classic Basil Pesto Sauce)...4
Easy, Herb-Packed Falafel..........................9
Make-Ahead Quinoa Salad.......................13
Fresh Herbs With Corn, Asparagus, and Chickpeas..15
Easy, Summery Zucchini-Basil Soup..........18
Grilled Corn, Tomato, Feta, and Herb Salad21
Shredded Chicken With Soba and Miso-Butter Sauce...23
DIY Chicken and Dill Instant Noodles........26
Spicy Peanut Noodle Salad.......................28
Easy Vegan Crispy Tofu Spring Rolls.........31
Grilled Chicken and Cabbage Salad With

Creamy Tahini Dressing............................35
Thai-Style Beef With Basil and Chilies......38
Isan-Style Spicy Thai Fried Pork Rind and Herb Salad..44
Grilled Vegetable and Jasmine Rice Salad. 46
Roman-Inspired Mixed-Green Salad..........49
Fresh Basil Mousse...................................54
Mint Chip Ice Cream.................................57

Tabbouleh Salad

There are lots of tabbouleh recipes in the world, but many give instructions that can lead to a sopping wet salad with bulgur that's too hard to eat. This one uses pre-salting steps to remove excess moisture from the tomatoes and parsley, then uses the water drained from the tomatoes to soak the bulgur until tender and flavorful. A hint of spices adds complexity and depth.

Why It Works

Pre-salting the tomatoes and parsley removes excess liquid through osmosis, preventing the salad from becoming soupy later.

Tomato water is re-infused into the salad by using it to soak the bulgur, enhancing the flavor.

Soaking the bulgur in heated tomato water ensures it will soften, regardless of its grind size.

Ingredients

3/4 pound ripe plum tomatoes, finely diced

2 cups finely chopped flat-leaf parsley leaves and tender stems (about 2 bunches), finely chopped with a sharp knife

2 teaspoons kosher salt, divided, plus more for seasoning

1/4 cup dry coarse bulgur wheat

1 cup finely chopped fresh mint leaves (about 1 bunch)

2 scallions, white and light green parts only, finely chopped

5 tablespoons extra-virgin olive oil

2 tablespoons fresh juice from 2 lemons

1/4 teaspoon ground coriander seed (optional; see note)

Pinch ground cinnamon (optional; see note)

Freshly ground black pepper

Romaine lettuce leaves, for serving

Directions

1. Season tomatoes with 1 teaspoon salt and toss to combine. Transfer to a fine mesh strainer or colander set in a bowl and allow to drain for 20 minutes. Reserve liquid.
2. Season parsley with remaining 1 teaspoon salt and toss to combine. Transfer to a large mixing bowl lined with paper towels and let stand for 20 minutes. Blot parsley with towels to remove excess moisture.
3. Bring 1/2 cup reserved tomato water to a boil, then pour over bulgur in a small heatproof bowl and let stand until bulgur is softened, about 1 hour (bulgur may still have a slight bite, but will continue to soften in the salad). Drain bulgur of any excess liquid and pat dry with paper towels.
4. In a large mixing bowl, stir together tomatoes, parsley, mint, bulgur, scallions, olive oil, lemon juice, coriander seed, and cinnamon until well combined. Season with salt and pepper. Serve tabbouleh with romaine leaves.

Special Equipment

Fine mesh strainer

Notes

Spices add complexity and depth to the tabbouleh, but you can omit or use different spices, as desired; allspice is another popular option.

Pesto alla Genovese (Classic Basil Pesto Sauce)

This pesto sauce, through rounds and rounds of testing, has been honed to the perfect ratio, ingredients, and method. And, while a mortar and pestle requires a bit of work, the superior sauce it produces compared to a food processor can't be argued with. This is the true, best pesto. Still, if you want to use a food processor, you will end up with a very good pesto using this ratio of ingredients. (Just pulse the garlic, salt, and pine nuts together first, then add the cheese and follow with the basil; stir in the oil.)

Why It Works

Using a mortar and pestle creates a luxurious sauce with a rich, deep flavor and a beautiful, silky texture that's superior to what a food processor can do.

Pecorino Fiore Sardo is a slightly milder sheep's-milk cheese, and creates a more balanced, less harsh pesto sauce.

Mild olive oil results in a more balanced, less aggressively spicy sauce.

Ingredients

2 medium cloves garlic

Coarse sea salt, as needed

3 ounces basil leaves (from about a 4-ounce bunch), washed with water still clinging to the leaves

2 tablespoons (30g) pine nuts

3/4 ounce (about 2 tablespoons) grated Parmigiano Reggiano

3/4 ounce (about 2 tablespoons) Pecorino Fiore Sardo (see note)

3/4 cup (175ml) mildly flavored extra-virgin olive oil

Directions

1. Using a mortar and pestle, combine garlic and sea salt and grind to a paste.

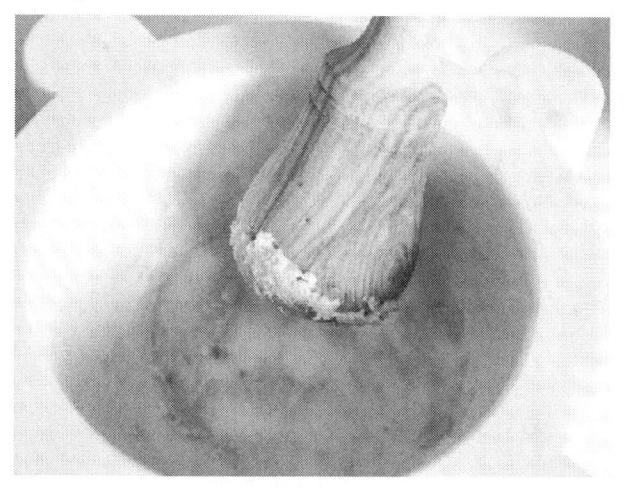

2. Add pine nuts and continue to crush with pestle, smashing and grinding them, until a sticky, only slightly chunky, beige paste forms.

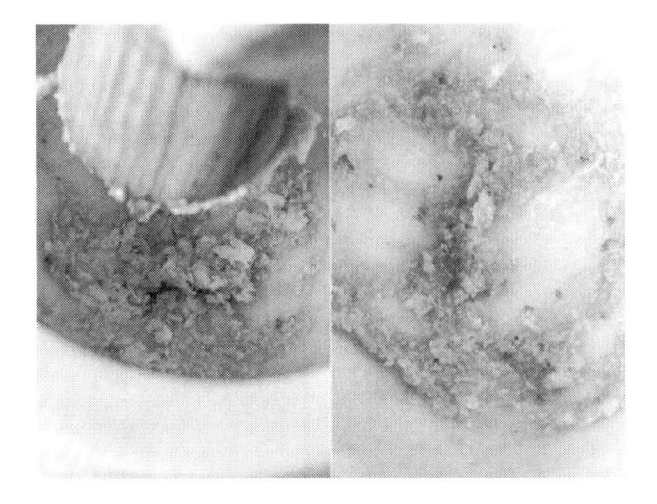

3. Add basil leaves, a handful at a time, and pound and grind against the walls of the mortar. Continue until all basil leaves have been crushed to fine bits.

4. Add both cheeses, then slowly drizzle in olive oil, working it into the pesto with the pestle until a fairly smooth, creamy, emulsified, sauce forms. Add more oil, if desired.

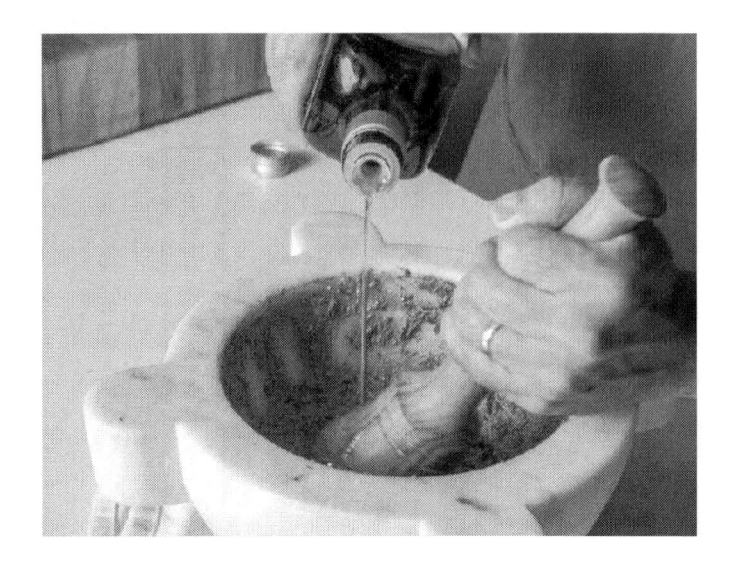

5. Pesto can be served with pasta right away, or transferred to a jar or container, covered with a small layer of olive oil, sealed, and refrigerated overnight.

Easy, Herb-Packed Falafel

Falafel often has good flavor, but a pasty, heavy texture. What I'm after is falafel that's shatteringly crisp on the outside and light, fluffy, almost crumbly on the inside, while still remaining very moist. Light enough that the balls can be eaten completely on their own without having to be shoved into a sandwich full of ingredients designed to distract you from their typical mushiness. (Of course, if you want them in a sandwich, they should hold up in there just as well.) I like my falafel to taste of chickpeas, but also to be packed with herb and spice flavor. Falafel that needs only simple condiments—tahini and hot sauce—to taste great.

Why It Works

Using dried chickpeas eliminates the need for flour or other binders, giving you falafel that is light and crisp.

Letting the falafel dough rest after grinding allows starch to seep out, making it easier for the balls to retain their shape.

Making small balls gives you a better ratio of crisp exterior to moist interior.

Ingredients

1/2 pound dried chickpeas (1 generous cup; 225g)

2 ounces picked fresh cilantro, parsley, or mint leaves, or preferably a mixture of all three (about 2 cups; 55g)

6 scallions, white and pale green parts only, sliced (about 2 ounces; 55g)

2 medium cloves garlic, minced (about 2 teaspoons; 10ml)

1 teaspoon (about 4g) ground cumin

1/2 teaspoon (about 2g) ground coriander seed

2 teaspoons (about 10g) kosher salt, plus more for seasoning

2 to 3 cups (480 to 720ml) vegetable oil, for frying

Tahini sauce, hummus, and/or zhug (Yemenite hot sauce) for serving

Directions

1. Rinse chickpeas and place in a large bowl. Cover with cold water, adding enough to allow the chickpeas to at least triple in volume. Cover and let stand at room temperature overnight. The next day, drain, rinse, and carefully dry chickpeas in a salad spinner.
2. Combine chickpeas, herbs, scallions, garlic, cumin, coriander, and salt in the work bowl of a food processor. Pulse until chickpeas are very finely minced, stopping the food processor to scrape down the sides as necessary. A handful of the mixture squeezed into a ball should be able to barely hold together. If not, process a little more.

3. Transfer mixture to a bowl, cover, and place in refrigerator for 15 minutes to allow time for more starch to seep out of chickpeas. This will help the balls retain their shape better once formed. Using a tablespoon measure, scoop out heaping spoonfuls of the mixture into your hand. Gently shape each into a ball (you will not be able to roll the mixture like cookie dough; this is okay) and place them on a clean plate.

4. When all the balls have been formed, fill a deep cast iron, carbon steel, or nonstick skillet or Dutch oven with 3/4 inch of oil. Heat over high heat until oil registers 375°F on an instant-read thermometer. Carefully lower chickpea balls into oil one at a time, allowing a little space between each ball and cooking

in batches if necessary. Adjust heat as necessary to maintain a temperature of between 350 and 375°F. Allow to cook undisturbed until well browned on bottom sides, then carefully flip balls with a fork until browned on second side, about 4 minutes total. Transfer cooked chickpea balls to a paper towel-lined plate and season with salt.

Repeat with remaining chickpea balls.

5. Serve immediately with tahini and/or hummus on the side, or stuffed into pita bread with tahini, tomatoes, cucumber, pickles, and shredded cabbage.

Make-Ahead Quinoa Salad

Loosely based on Middle Eastern tabbouleh salad, this easy make-ahead salad combines grape tomatoes (sweet and ripe any time of year) with cucumber, parsley, mint, and quinoa for a bright and refreshing make-ahead salad that's hearty enough to serve as a light meal.

Ingredients

1 cup quinoa

1 pint grape tomatoes, split into quarters

1 large cucumber, seeds removed, cut into 1/2-inch pieces

Kosher salt

2 small shallots, minced

1/2 cup roughly chopped flat-leaf parsley leaves

1/4 cup roughly chopped fresh mint leaves

5 tablespoons extra-virgin olive oil

2 tablespoons red wine vinegar

Freshly ground black pepper

Directions

1. Combine quinoa and 2 cups water in a small saucepan. Bring to

a boil, stir, reduce heat to low, cover, and cook for 7 minutes. Shut off heat and let rest until water is absorbed, about 5 minutes longer. Transfer quinoa to a fine mesh strainer and rinse under cold water until thoroughly chilled. Let drain for 10 minutes.
2. While quinoa cooks, combine tomatoes and cucumbers in a colander set in the sink. Season with salt and toss to coat. Let drain in sink until ready to combine with quinoa.
3. In a large bowl, toss drained quinoa, drained tomatoes and cucumbers, shallots, parsley, mint, olive oil, and red wine vinegar. Season to taste with salt and pepper. Serve immediately, or for best flavor, let rest overnight in a sealed container in the refrigerator. Salad can be stored in a sealed container in the refrigerator for up to 5 days

Fresh Herbs With Corn, Asparagus, and Chickpeas

When summer hits, one of my favorite dishes is tabbouleh, its bright and fresh aroma from the various chopped herbs interspersed with airy bites of bulgur. Here, I swap the bulgur for chickpeas that are crisped in a pan with shallots, a generous hit of cumin, freshly shucked corn kernels and bite-sized asparagus. Combined with the chopped herbs and topped with sumac-filled yogurt, it makes a nutrient-packed, fresh summer dish that hits the table in less than 30 minutes.

Why this recipe works:

Keeping the fine herb stems adds extra crunch to the salad.

Dressing the herbs ahead of time allows the flavors to soak in.

Sumac has a subtle citrus flavor that blends well with yogurt.

Ingredients

1 bunch fresh parsley, thick stems discarded and roughly chopped

1 bunch fresh cilantro, thick stems discarded and roughly chopped

1 1/2 cups fresh dill, thick stems discarded and roughly chopped

1 1/2 cups fresh mint, thick stems discarded and roughly chopped

4 tablespoons extra-virgin olive oil, divided

4 tablespoons fresh lemon juice from 2 lemons, plus more as needed, divided

Kosher salt and freshly ground black pepper

1 shallot, thinly sliced

1 tablespoon ground cumin

1 teaspoon cayenne

2 ears of corn, kernels sliced off (about 1 1/3 cups)

1 bunch asparagus, woody ends discarded and cut into 2-inch pieces (about 2 cups)

1 (15-ounce) can chickpeas, drained and rinsed

1 (7-ounce) container Greek yogurt, preferably 2%

1 tablespoon sumac

Directions

1. Combine the parsley, cilantro, dill, and mint in a large serving bowl and stir in 2 tablespoons olive oil and 2 tablespoons lemon juice. Season with salt and pepper and set aside.
2. In a 12-inch skillet, heat remaining 2 tablespoons oil over medium-high heat until shimmering. Add shallots and a pinch of salt, cooking until softened, about 2 minutes. Add cumin and cayenne, stirring, until fragrant, about 30 seconds longer. Add corn, asparagus, and chickpeas and season with salt and pepper. Continue to cook, stirring occasionally, until vegetables are tender, about 7 minutes. Remove from heat and allow to cool slightly.
3. Stir together yogurt and sumac in a small bowl. In a serving bowl, combine cooked vegetables and chickpeas with herbs. Season with salt and pepper and add more lemon juice, if necessary. Serve with yogurt alongside.

Cooking with Herbs

Easy, Summery Zucchini-Basil Soup

The great thing about this zucchini-basil soup is that it cooks so darn quickly. Zucchini is a very watery vegetable, with a weak, almost spongy structure that breaks down rapidly during cooking. This is frequently an obstacle when you're preparing zucchini, but here, it's a positive: It means we can cook the zucchini until it's tender enough to blend, while retaining its bright green color for a soup that's both tasty and attractive.

Why It Works

Leeks are a mild onion that complement mild zucchini perfectly.

Adding basil in two stages gives you layers of basil flavor.

Ingredients

2 tablespoons (30ml) extra-virgin olive oil, plus more as needed and to serve

1 large leek, finely diced (about 8 ounces; 225g)

3 medium ribs celery, finely diced (about 6 ounces; 170g)

Kosher salt

3 medium cloves garlic, minced (about 3/4 ounce; 25g)

1 1/2 pounds (700g) zucchini, split lengthwise and cut into 1/2-inch disks (see note)

2 cups packed fresh basil leaves, roughly chopped (about 2 ounces; 55g), divided

5 cups (1.2L) water

Freshly ground black pepper

Fresh juice from 1 lemon, to taste

Directions

1. Heat olive oil in a large saucepan or saucier over medium heat until shimmering. Add leek and celery. Season with salt and cook, stirring, until vegetables are softened but not browned, about 5 minutes. If pan starts to look dry at any point, add a small splash of olive oil. Add garlic and cook, stirring, until fragrant, about 30 seconds. Add zucchini and cook, stirring, for 1 minute. Add half of basil, stir to combine, and add water.
2. Bring to a simmer and cook, stirring occasionally, until zucchini is tender but still bright green, about 10 minutes. Add remaining half of basil and blend soup using a handheld immersion blender or a countertop blender until it is as rough or as smooth as you like it. Season to taste with salt, black pepper, and lemon juice and serve, drizzling with additional olive oil at the table.

Cooking with Herbs

Grilled Corn, Tomato, Feta, and Herb Salad

This is one of my favorite salads of all time and an absolute classic: corn grilled until it's smoky and sweet, then tossed with ripe end-of-season tomatoes in a light lemon and olive oil dressing. Salty chunks of feta and a ton of fresh herbs finish it off. As simple and delicious as recipes come.

Why this recipe works:

The big secret is not so secret at all: get the best darned end-of-summer produce you can find, and put it together.

Heavily charring the corn brings out its natural sweetness.

The lemon and olive oil dressing is a simple as it gets, and lets the vegetables' natural flavors come through.

Ingredients

3 tablespoons best quality extra-virgin olive oil

1 tablespoon juice from 1 lemon

4 ears sweet corn, husks removed

2 pounds ripe tomatoes (see note), cut into bite-size chunks

1/4 cup roughly chopped fresh flat-leaf parsley leaves

1/4 cup roughly chopped fresh basil leaves

1/4 cup roughly chopped fresh mint leaves

8 ounces feta cheese, cut into 1/2-inch chunks

Kosher salt and freshly ground black pepper

Directions

1. Combine olive oil and lemon juice in a small bowl and whisk to combine. Set aside.

3. Light one chimney full of charcoal. When all the charcoal is lit and covered with gray ash, pour out and arrange the coals on one side of the charcoal grate. Set cooking grate in place, cover grill and allow to preheat for 5 minutes. Alternatively, set half the burners on a gas grill to the highest heat setting, cover, and preheat for 10 minutes. Clean and oil the grilling grate. To char corn without a grill, see note.
4. Place corn directly over hot side of grill and cook, turning occasionally, until charred on all sides and fully tender, about 10 minutes total. Remove corn from grill and allow to rest until cool enough to handle, about 5 minutes.
5. Working one ear at a time, hold the corn vertically inside a large bowl and use a sharp knife to remove the kernels. Discard the cob. Add tomatoes, parsley, basil, mint, and feta cheese to the bowl. Whisk the dressing and add it to the bowl. Season with salt and pepper and gently fold with clean hands until all the ingredients are incorporated and coated in the dressing. Serve immediately.

Shredded Chicken With Soba and Miso-Butter Sauce

I think there should be a t-shirt or sign that reads: Miso butter just makes it all better. Not soba noodles, shredded chicken, and crunchy vegetables come together in one pot. It take half an hour to make from start to finish, but it'll only take a fraction of that time to slurp it all up whether you use chopsticks or forks.

Combining salty, deeply savory miso with butter creates an intensely rich sauce with a nutty aroma that works perfectly for coating noodles and tender shreds of chicken. The kicker for the recipe is that I use skin-on chicken thighs that brown in the pan, releasing bits of char as well as tasty drippings that are later used as the cooking liquid for the soba noodles.

The hot noodles are tossed with the miso-butter combo and quickly absorb its addictive flavor. I top it off with scallions, cilantro, and crunchy bean sprouts for that necessary hit of fresh crunch.

Why this recipe works:

Searing the chicken first ensures extra flavor and tasty drippings in the pot.

Cooking the soba in chicken drippings adds tons of flavor.

Miso butter makes it all better.

Ingredients

1 pound bone-in, skin on chicken thighs (about 3 thighs)

Kosher salt and freshly ground black pepper

3 cups homemade or store-bought low-sodium chicken stock

2 tablespoons extra-virgin olive oil

1/2 stick (4 tablespoons) unsalted butter at room temperature

1 tablespoon white miso paste

3 bundles dried soba noodles (about 6 ounces)

2 scallions, thinly sliced, white and light green parts

1/2 cup picked cilantro leaves

1 cup picked bean sprouts

1 lemon, cut into wedges

Directions

1. Season the chicken with salt and pepper. Heat the oil in a large pot over medium-high heat until shimmering. Cook the chicken, skin-side down, until crisp, about 7 minutes. Flip and cook until the second side has browned, about 4 minutes more. Add the broth, adjust the heat to maintain a simmer, cover, and cook until the chicken has cooked through, about 12 minutes more. Meanwhile, mix the butter and miso together in a small bowl.
2. Transfer the chicken to a plate and shred with a fork and knife. Discard skin and bones. Bring the broth to a hard boil over high heat. Add the noodles and cook according to the package instructions. Drain, reserving broth for another use if desired, and immediately toss in a serving bowl with the miso-butter. Toss to coat, then add in the chicken. Top with scallions, cilantro and sprouts. Serve immediately with lemon wedges

Cooking with Herbs

DIY Chicken and Dill Instant Noodles

This pot of noodles, flavored with roast chicken, peas, and onions, can be made ahead and taken to work. Just add boiling water, seal it up for three minutes, add the contents of the fresh-herb packet, and you've got a hot lunch ready.

Why It Works

All the convenience of a package of instant noodles, but with better ingredients and better flavor.

By keeping the dill separate from the rest of the ingredients, you can stir it into the hot soup for bright, fresh, layered flavor.

Shredded rotisserie chicken, rice noodles (or par-cooked ramen or Italian noodles), and frozen peas make for quick and easy prep.

Ingredients

4 tablespoons (60ml) high-quality chicken base, such as Better Than Bouillon

1 cup frozen peas

1 small onion, thinly sliced

12 ounces (340g) shredded chicken meat from 1 rotisserie chicken

4 small nests rice noodles or precooked ramen or Italian pasta (see note)

Kosher salt and freshly ground black pepper

1/2 cup minced fresh dill leaves

Directions

1. Divide chicken base, peas, onion, chicken, and noodles evenly between 4 resealable glass jars. Season lightly with salt and pepper. Divide dill between 4 small zipper-lock bags and seal bags, squeezing out all of the air. Tuck bags into jars and seal. Refrigerate for up to 4 days.

2. When ready to serve, remove dill packet and add boiling water to the top of the jar. Seal jar and let sit 2 minutes. Open jar, stir in dill, and serve.

Spicy Peanut Noodle Salad

Ingredients

8 ounces fresh Chinese noodles (see note)

For the Dressing:

1/2 cup chunky peanut butter

3 tablespoons soy sauce

3 tablespoons fresh ground chili sauce (such as Huy Fong brand Sambal Oelek or Sriracha), more or less to taste

2 tablespoons juice from 2 limes (or rice wine vinegar)

1 tablespoon toasted sesame seed oil

1 clove garlic, grated on a microplane grater

1 tablespoon sugar or honey

3 tablespoons warm water

To Assemble:

2 large red, orange, or yellow bell peppers, sliced into thin strips

1 large cucumber, seeded and sliced into fine julienne or small half moons

1 cup mung bean sprouts

1 cup loosely packed fresh basil, mint, or cilantro leaves

8 scallions, finely sliced at a severe bias to create long, thin strips

2 jalapeño peppers, seeds and ribs removed, sliced into fine strips

1 to 2 red thai bird chilis, finely minced (optonal)

1/2 cup roughly crushed roasted peanuts

Directions

1. Cook noodles according to package directions. Drain and transfer to a large bowl of ice water. Agitate noodles until thoroughly chilled. Set aside while you make the dressing.
2. In a large bowl, combine peanut butter, soy sauce, chili sauce, lime juice, sesame seed oil, garlic, sugar or honey, and water. Whisk until homogeneous. Drain noodles thoroughly and add to bowl. Add bell peppers, cucumber, bean sprouts, basil leaves, scallions, jalapeños, and bird chilis (if using). Toss to combine. Serve immediately, topped with roasted peanuts.

Easy Vegan Crispy Tofu Spring Rolls

The real key to these great spring rolls is to balance the textures and flavors of the ingredients inside the soft, stretchy rice paper wrapper. For this version, I'm using tender pea shoots, along with carrots cut into a fine julienne, crispy marinated tofu, herbs, chilies, and toasted peanuts.

Why It Works

Slow-cooking the tofu gets it extra crisp and ready to absorb flavor from the marinade.

A combination of hearty textures and fresh flavors makes this dish light but satisfying.

Ingredients

1 (14-ounce; 400g) block firm (non-silken) tofu, cut into matchsticks approximately 2 inches long and 1/2 inch square

3 tablespoons (45ml) vegetable oil

1 recipe Peanut-Tamarind Dipping Sauce

1 large carrot, peeled and cut into a fine julienne

4 ounces pea greens

2 cups mixed picked fresh herbs, such as cilantro, mint, and Thai basil

Chopped toasted peanuts

Finely sliced Thai bird or serrano chili peppers

20 dried spring roll rice paper wrappers

Directions

1. Place tofu in a large colander and set in the sink. Pour 1 quart boiling water over tofu and let rest for 1 minute. Transfer to a paper towel–lined tray and press dry. Heat vegetable oil in a large nonstick or cast iron skillet over medium-low heat until shimmering. Add tofu and cook, turning occasionally, until golden brown and crisp on all surfaces, about 10 minutes total. Transfer to a paper towel–lined plate to drain.
2. Transfer drained tofu to a large bowl and add 5 tablespoons peanut-tamarind sauce. Toss to coat tofu.
3. Transfer tofu, carrots, greens, herbs, peanuts, peppers, and remaining dipping sauce to serving platters. Serve with rice

paper wrappers and a bowl of warm water. To eat, dip a rice paper wrapper in warm water until moist on all surfaces, then transfer to your plate. Place a small amount of desired fillings in the center. Roll the front edge of the wrapper over the filling away from you, then fold the right side over toward the center. Continue rolling until a tight roll with one open end has formed. Dip spring roll in dipping sauce as you eat.

Grilled Chicken and Cabbage Salad With Creamy Tahini Dressing

I've been trying to come up with great ways to use leftover grilled chicken breasts that mask their inherent dryness and give them new life. One of my favorites is a fresh, crunchy salad with cabbage, red onion, and a ton of fresh herbs in a tahini-based dressing.

Why It Works

Massaging the chicken meat with olive oil and lemon juice before adding the remaining ingredients gives it more flavor, while also tenderizing it.

A ton of fresh herbs makes the salad taste light and refreshing, though it's still hearty enough to eat as a light meal.

Ingredients

3/4 pound leftover grilled chicken breasts (about 2 breasts) or 3/4 pound picked cooked rotisserie chicken meat, shredded

5 tablespoons extra-virgin olive oil, divided

3 tablespoons fresh juice from 2 lemons, divided

4 medium cloves garlic, finely minced (about 4 teaspoons), divided

Kosher salt and freshly ground black pepper

3/4 pound finely shredded red cabbage (about 1/2 head)

1 small red onion, thinly sliced

1/3 cup tahini paste

1/2 cup roughly chopped fresh mint leaves

1/2 cup roughly chopped fresh parsley leaves

1/2 cup roughly chopped fresh cilantro leaves

1 tablespoon roasted sesame seeds

Directions

1. Combine chicken with 2 tablespoons olive oil, 1 tablespoon lemon juice, and 1 teaspoon minced garlic in a large bowl. Season with salt and pepper and massage with clean hands to work the dressing into the chicken. Add cabbage and red onion and toss to combine. Set aside.
2. In a small bowl, combine tahini, remaining 2 tablespoons lemon juice, and remaining 3 teaspoons minced garlic. Whisking constantly, drizzle in remaining 3 tablespoons olive oil. Slowly whisk in up to 1/2 cup water until a thick, pancake-batter-like consistency is reached. Season to taste with salt and pepper.
3. Add mint, parsley, and cilantro to bowl with shredded chicken and cabbage, along with half of sesame seeds and all of the dressing. Toss with clean hands to combine. Adjust to taste with more salt, pepper, or lemon juice as necessary. Transfer to serving platter or bowl and sprinkle with remaining sesame seeds. Serve immediately. Salad can be stored in a covered container in the refrigerator for up to 3 days.

Thai-Style Beef With Basil and Chilies

Phat ka-phrao is a ubiquitous street dish in Thailand, where cooks wielding woks will rapidly stir-fry sliced or minced meat flavored with garlic, shallots, fish sauce, and fiery Thai bird chilies, finish it off with a big handful of holy basil, and serve it with rice and perhaps a fried egg on top. Holy basil, though, is difficult to come by in the United States; Thai purple basil, on the other hand, is not. So instead of a recipe for phat ka-phrao, here is a recipe for phat bai horapha, which is still darned delicious.

Why It Works

Using a mortar and pestle to smash the chilies and garlic brings out more of their flavor than chopping or grinding in a food processor.

Browning the beef in batches lets you sear the meat without steaming it or overcooking it.

Ingredients

1 pound (450g) flank steak, skirt steak, hanger steak, or flap meat, cut into 1/4-inch-thick strips

1 tablespoon (15ml) soy sauce, divided

5 teaspoons (25ml) Asian fish sauce, divided

1 teaspoon (4g) white sugar

4 to 6 fresh red or green Thai bird chilies, divided

6 medium cloves garlic, divided

1 1/2 tablespoons (20g) palm sugar (see note)

1 small shallot, thinly sliced

4 makrut lime leaves, very thinly sliced into hairs (central vein discarded), plus more for garnish (see note)

2 tablespoons (30ml) vegetable or canola oil, divided

2 cups packed Thai purple basil (about 2 ounces; 55g)(see note)

Dried Thai chili flakes or red pepper flakes to taste (optional)

1/4 cup fried shallots (see note)

Kosher salt

Cooked rice, for serving

Directions

1. Combine beef, 1 teaspoon soy sauce, 2 teaspoons fish sauce, and white sugar in a bowl. Toss to combine and set in refrigerator to marinate for at least 15 minutes and up to overnight.
2. Roughly chop half of Thai chilies and garlic and place inside a stone mortar with palm sugar. Grind with pestle until a mostly smooth paste has formed. Add remaining fish sauce and soy sauce and mash in mortar to form a sauce. Set aside. Finely slice remaining garlic and chilies and combine with shallot and lime leaves in a small bowl.

3. When ready to cook, heat 1 tablespoon oil in a wok over high heat until smoking. Add half of beef and cook, without moving, until well seared, about 1 minute. Continue cooking, while stirring and tossing, until beef is lightly cooked but still pink in spots, about 1 minute. Transfer to a large bowl. Repeat with 1 more tablespoon oil and remaining beef, transferring beef to the same bowl. Wipe out wok.

4. Reheat wok over high heat and add all of the beef, along with sliced garlic/chili/makrut lime mixture. Continue to cook, tossing and stirring constantly, until stir-fry is aromatic and shallots have completely softened, about 1 minute.

5. Add sauce mixture to wok and cook, tossing and stirring constantly, until completely reduced. (The beef should look moist, but there should be no liquid in the bottom of the wok.) Immediately add basil and toss to combine. Season to taste with salt and and optional Thai chili or red pepper flakes. Transfer to a serving platter. Top with more makrut lime threads and fried shallots. Serve immediately with rice.

Isan-Style Spicy Thai Fried Pork Rind and Herb Salad

The dressing for this salad fires on all cylinders with big bursts of hot, acidic, sweet, and savory elements all in balance. The dressing coats crisp fried pork rinds, softening them up slightly, and making them taste almost bright and refreshing when coupled with plenty of fresh herbs and bean sprouts.

Why this recipe works:

A combination of both dried and fresh Thai chilies, sugar, fish sauce, and lime juice make a dressing that is bold and delicious.

Pounding the garlic and chilies in a mortar and pestle releases more flavors than a food processor or hand-chopping do.

Packaged fried pork rinds absorb a ton of flavor from the dressing.

Ingredients

1 small red onion, split in half from pole to pole and thinly sliced

2 scallions, thinly sliced on a sharp bias

3 medium cloves garlic

2 teaspoons Thai red pepper flakes (more or less to taste, see note)

1 small green thai chili or 1/2 small Serrano chili, finely chopped

1 tablespoon brown sugar (more or less to taste)

1 tablespoon Asian fish sauce (more or less to taste)

1 tablespoon juice from 1 lime (more or less to taste)

1 roma tomato, split in half and thinly sliced

1 cup mung bean sprouts, washed, trimmed, and dried

2 (1.75 ounces) packages unflavored fried pork rinds

1/2 cup fresh picked mint leaves

1/2 cup fresh picked cilantro leaves

Lime wedges, for serving

Directions

1. Place onions and scallions in a bowl, cover with cold water, add 6 ice cubes, and place in refrigerator until ready to use, at least 5 minutes.
2. Combine garlic, pepper flakes, and Thai chilies in a mortar and pestle and pound into a fine paste (see note). Add sugar, fish sauce, and lime juice, and pound until the sugar is dissolved. Taste dressing and add more sugar, fish sauce, lime juice, or pepper flakes to taste. It should be strongly spicy, sweet, salty, and acidic.
3. Combine tomatoes, bean sprouts, pork rinds, mint, cilantro, and dressing in a large bowl and toss to combine. Carefully drain onions and scallions. Add to bowl and toss to combine. Serve immediately.

Grilled Vegetable and Jasmine Rice Salad

Inspired by Thai grilled bef salad (neua nam tok), this salad replaces the meat with grilled vegetables and adds fragrant jasmine rice. It's loaded with fresh herbs and dressed with a bracing, fish sauce-spiked lime vinaigrette. Plus, because the vegetables are grilled, they give the salad a deeper, smoky flavor.

Note: Do not overcook the rice. You want it to stand up to the vinaigrette without turning into a soggy mess. It's therefore best to remove it from the heat right when it loses its "bite."

Ingredients

For the Vinaigrette:

1/2 cup fresh lime juice from about 8 to 10 limes

1 1/2 tablespoons fish sauce

1 1/2 tablespoons brown sugar

2 medium cloves garlic, minced

1 1/2 teaspoons Sriracha

2 tablespoons vegetable oil

For the Salad:

2 (3/4-inch-thick) slices from a large red onion

3 large carrots, peeled and quartered lengthwise

15 sugar-snap peas

8 whole tri-color mini bell peppers or 1 large red or yellow bell pepper, quartered

2 jalapeños

2 tablespoons vegetable oil

Kosher salt and freshly gound black pepper

1/4 cup finely chopped cilantro leaves and tender stems

1/4 cup finely chopped fresh mint

1/4 cup finely chopped Thai basil or sweet basil

2 cups cooked and cooled Jasmine rice (see note)

1/2 cup lightly toasted cashews

Directions

1. For the Vinaigrette: Whisk ingredients together in a small bowl. Reserve.
2. For the Salad: Light one chimney full of charcoal. When all the charcoal is lit and covered with gray ash, pour out and arrange the coals on one side of the charcoal grate. Set cooking grate in place, cover grill, and allow to preheat for 5 minutes. Alternatively, set half the burners on a gas grill to the highest heat setting, cover, and preheat for 10 minutes. Clean and oil the grilling grate.
3. Toss onion slices, carrots, snap peas, peppers, and jalapeños with oil in a large bowl. Season with salt and pepper. Thread snap peas on one skewer; thread mini bell peppers, if using, and jalapeños on second skewer.
4. Grill vegetables directly over the flames, turning once, until browned on both sides, about 4 minutes total.
5. When snap peas, peppers, and jalapeños are cool enough to handle, remove skewers. Stem and seed peppers and jalapeños, and discard stems and fibrous strings from snap peas. Chop vegetables coarsely, place in a large bowl and toss

with 2 tablespoons of vinaigrette. Let stand for 5 minutes. Then, add cilantro, mint, basil, rice, and cashews and toss well. Dress with vinaigrette to taste and toss well again. Serve slightly warm of at room temperature, passing additional vinaigrette at the table.

Roman-Inspired Mixed-Green Salad

Want a truly great mixed green salad full of vibrant lettuces, flavorful herbs, and bitter greens? You're not going to find it in the pre-mixed salad section of your supermarket. Instead, make your own with the freshest whole heads of lettuce, radicchio, herbs, dandelion, and more. This incredibly simple recipe is inspired by the Roman salad called misticanza, which traditionally combines several wild greens. It's unlikely most of us outside of Rome can find those greens, but we can capture the same spirit by combining a good mix of tender, bitter, and herbaceous greens.

Why It Works

A good mix of the freshest leafy greens delivers a flavorful salad with personality.

Using what's seasonal and available to you means the salad will always be at its best.

A light dressing of good olive oil and lemon juice is all top-quality greens need.

Ingredients

Mixed of wild and/or cultivated leafy greens and tender fresh herbs, such as lettuces, chicory, endive, raddichio, dandelion, purslane, frisée, kale, fennel fronds, parsley, tarragon, chervil, basil, mint, and more, preferably grown locally and at peak season and freshness (see note)

Extra-virgin olive oil

Fresh lemon juice

Kosher or sea salt

Directions

1. Pick over the leafy vegetables, discarding any wilted or damaged leaves. Cut lettuce leaves free of their cores, pick the tender herbs from stems, and quarter, core, and slice tight leafy heads like radicchio and endive. Wash everything in several changes of water until no dirt or grit remains. Dry well in a salad spinner.
3. In a large serving bowl, gently toss salad with just enough olive oil to gently coat leaves. Add a splash of lemon juice and salt to taste, tossing to combine. Serve.

Warm Couscous Salad

Flakes of salmon and wilted spinach add body and flavor to this warm couscous salad that's seasoned with mustard and dill. Ready in under 30 minutes, it's perfect for a quick weeknight meal or picnic lunch.

Why this recipe works:

Cooking the salmon first allows it to rest while the couscous cooks.

Making the dressing in the serving bowl means one less dish to wash.

Ingredients

2 (8-ounce) salmon filets, preferably wild

Kosher salt and freshly ground black pepper

1/3 cup plus 2 tablespoons extra-virgin olive oil, divided

1 medium shallot, thinly sliced

6 ounces pearled couscous

3 cups homemade vegetable stock or store-bought low-sodium vegetable broth

2 tablespoons Dijon mustard

2 tablespoons fresh juice from 1 lemon

1/2 cup picked dill, roughly chopped, plus more for garnish

1 1/2 cups spinach leaves, chopped in half if large, or left whole if baby

Directions

1. Season salmon with salt and pepper. Heat 1/3 cup of oil in a 12-inch stainless steel skillet over medium-high heat until shimmering. Add salmon, skin-side down, and immediately reduce the heat to medium-low. Cook, pressing down gently with a spatula to ensure contact, until the skin is rendered and crisp, about 6 minutes. If skin shows resistance when attempting to lift with a spatula, allow it to continue to cook

until it lifts easily.

2. Flip salmon and cook until an instant-read thermometer inserted into the thickest part registers 120°F for medium rare or 130°F for medium, about 1 minute longer. Transfer salmon to a paper towel-lined plate and allow to cool. Once cooled, flake salmon using your hands; discard skin.

3. Meanwhile, wipe out the skillet. Add the remaining 2 tablespoons of oil and heat over medium-high heat until shimmering. Add shallot and a pinch of salt and cook until softened, about 2 minutes. Add couscous and cook, stirring, until lightly toasted and fragrant, about 1 minute. Add broth, stirring to combine, and adjust the heat to maintain a simmer. Cook until most of the liquid has been absorbed and the couscous is tender. Strain any excess liquid.

4. In a large serving bowl, mix together mustard and lemon juice. Stir in couscous, along with dill and spinach, stirring to fluff the couscous and wilt the spinach. Stir in flaked salmon and season with salt and pepper. Garnish with dill and serve right away.

Fresh Basil Mousse

The flavor and color of this emerald green mousse comes from fresh basil, ground to a pulp with sugar, then steeped into an eggless custard base. White chocolate plays a supporting role, adding richness and body, while melding seamlessly with the herbal aroma. It's as creamy and light as a mousse should be, and the perfect showcase for fresh summer fruit, like strawberries, apricots, and nectarines.

Why It Works

White chocolate gives the eggless mousse richness and body.

Briefly infusing, then straining, the basil into the base prevents bitterness while keeping the mousse creamy and smooth.

A piping bag makes the mousse easy to portion while it's runny and soft.

Ingredients

To Bloom the Gelatin:

1/4 ounce unflavored gelatin powder, such as Knox or Now Foods (about 2 1/4 teaspoons; 7g)

1 ounce cold milk, any percentage will do (about 2 tablespoons; 30g)

For the Mousse:

3 1/2 ounces plain or toasted sugar (about 1/2 cup; 100g)

1 1/2 ounces fresh basil (about 1 1/2 cups, loosely packed; 43g)

1 teaspoon (4g) Diamond Crystal kosher salt; for table salt, use about half as much by volume or the same weight

4 ounces roughly chopped white chocolate, not chips (about 2/3 cup; 115g)

12 ounces milk, divided, any percentage will do (about 1 1/2 cups;

340g)

8 ounces heavy cream (about 1 cup; 225g)

Fresh fruit, such as sliced strawberries, apricots, or nectarines, for garnish

Pine nuts or slivered almonds, for garnish (optional)

Directions

1. To Bloom the Gelatin: In a small ramekin, mix gelatin with milk, stirring with a fork to break up the lumps.
2. Meanwhile, for the Mousse: In the bowl of a food processor, combine sugar and basil, then grind until reduced to wet pulp. In a 2-quart stainless steel saucier, combine basil-sugar with salt, white chocolate, and approximately one-third of the milk. Warm over medium heat, stirring constantly with a flexible spatula, until the white chocolate has fully dissolved and the mixture is hot to the touch, but not simmering. Remove from heat, add prepared gelatin, and stir until fully melted.
3. Using a fine-mesh strainer set over a large heat-proof bowl, strain mixture, pressing on the basil solids with a flexible spatula to extract as much liquid as possible without forcing the pulp through the sieve; discard basil solids. Stir in the remaining milk, then cover and refrigerate until firm and cold, about 3 hours or to a temperature of 40°F (4°C). Alternatively,

the mixture can be refrigerated for up to 12 hours.
4. In the bowl of a stand mixer fitted with a paddle attachment, beat the chilled base on medium speed until creamy and smooth, about 90 seconds; if needed, use a flexible spatula to remove any remaining lumps by smearing them against the side of the bowl. Scrape the smooth base back into its original bowl.
5. Add the cream to the stand mixer bowl (no need to wash) and whip with the whisk attachment until thick and stiff, about 3 minutes, although this will vary depending on the power of the mixer. Once thick, roughly fold approximately half the whipped cream into the basil mixture; then add the remainder and fold gently to combine. Transfer to a disposable pastry bag, snip off 1/4-inch from the tip, then pipe into serving dishes. Cover and refrigerate until firm, about 1 hour, or until needed, up to 12 hours. Serve with fresh fruit, sliced and macerated with sugar to taste, and/or nuts if you'd like.

Mint Chip Ice Cream

No mint leaves can match the charged blast of a slug of mint extract, but fresh mint ice cream has an unbeatable roundness of flavor you just can't find in a bottle. Add in lacy straciatella swirls that don't turn brittle like regular frozen chocolate for a mint chip ice cream that'll put all the others to bed.

Why It Works

Steeping fresh mint leaves in hot cream and milk for 2 hours is ideal for extracting that minty-fresh flavor.

Chocolate blended with a little oil, then drizzled into the churning ice cream, melts smooth and creamy on the tongue, unlike the typical chocolate chunks.

Ingredients

2 cups heavy cream

1 cup whole milk

1 large or two small bunches fresh mint leaves

6 egg yolks

1/2 cup sugar

1/2 teaspoon kosher salt, or to taste

4 ounces dark chocolate

2 teaspoons neutral-flavored oil, such as vegetable or canola

Directions

1. In a heavy-bottomed saucepan, bring cream and milk to a simmer. Remove from heat, stir in mint leaves, cover, and let steep for 2 hours.
2. In another heavy-bottomed saucepan, whisk together egg yolks and sugar until well combined. Quickly strain dairy into pot with egg yolks, pressing on the mint with the back of a spoon to extract as much mint flavor as possible. Whisk until fully

combined, then set over medium heat and cook, whisking frequently, until a custard forms on a spoon and a finger swiped across the back leaves a clean line, or until custard temperature reaches 170°F. Add salt to taste.
3. Pour custard through a fine mesh strainer into an airtight container and chill in an ice bath or refrigerator until temperature drops to 40°F, about 4 hours for ice bath, up to overnight for refrigerator.
4. Churn ice cream according to manufacturer's instructions. While ice cream churns, melt chocolate in a microwave or double boiler and stir to combine with oil. During final minutes of churning, slowly drizzle chocolate into ice cream to form thin, lacy lines, pausing to break up larger chocolate chunks with a spoon, if needed. Transfer churned ice cream to an airtight container and harden in freezer for at least 4 hours before serving.

Printed in Great Britain
by Amazon